ENDORSEMENTS

In *Still Voices* the sensitive reader will encounter a wide range of place and time—from standing by a pond at dawn before beginning farm work, to hearing the ancient echo of liturgy in a stone abbey. The contemplative reader will find sacred space in the author's interior reading of Psalms. All will know that Sheldon Clark is a person of faith, whose deep engagement with sacred text opens to the voice of Divine Providence, which we, too, are able to hear. This is a beautiful book—there is a black and white image on every page to provide exquisite visual setting for each poem. I heartily endorse *Still Voices* as poetry to lighten our path.

Rev. F. Gardiner Perry, D. Min.
Member of the Board of Trustees of
The Center for Swedenborgian Studies at
The Graduate Theological Union
Berkeley, California

Sheldon Clark's volume *Still Voices* offers a sensitive articulation for such a time as this. His meditative style is rooted in ancient scripture but offers a comforting wisdom that our generation needs to hear. In his poetry Clark awakens our senses to inhabit the subtle movements of nature. Honest to the rhythms of life this volume arouses the wisdom of a contemporary sage who, in his poetry, guides us on the spiritual paths of grace. Reading the poems in this volume evokes the joy and sorrow, the triumphs and tragedies of life. Readers will find it to be spiritually uplifting as they connect with the expression of an interior vision of life with God. I am so pleased to have gained the acquaintance of the author and to celebrate the publication of this book of poetry. I hope others will find its refreshment and spiritual nurture in the way that I did.

Phil C. Zylla, D.Th.
Vice President, Academic
Professor of Pastoral Theology
J. Gordon and Margaret Warnock Jones Chair in Church and Ministry
McMaster Divinity College

PREFACE

I believe that poetry results from observation, experience, emotional and spiritual wells, ideas, disciplined learning, nature, reflections and reflective thinking, uninhibited free association, residual pools of cultural imbibing, the multi-faceted light flashes of environmental exposure, inspiration, and that inexplicable overriding compulsion to set it down in intensive language.

I believe in the power of Divine Providence to lead us from the celestial vistas of mountain tops to the depths "of the valleys of evil." No subject is forbidden to the art of the imagination to ponder and to record what is and the hope of what possibilities might be. My experience with the poetic process is that a poem does not necessarily materialize "full blown from the head of Zeus." Rather, writing poetry tends to develop over time and usually requires careful consideration to uncover *le mot juste* exactly for this precise moment in time and space.

Sheldon H. Clark

Copyright © 2020, 2021 by Sheldon H. Clark.
All rights reserved

Published by Rock's Mills Press, Oakville, Ontario
www.rocksmillspress.com
For information, please contact us at customer.service@rocksmillspress.com.

ACKNOWLEDGEMENTS

I gratefully acknowledge the thoughtful insights offered to this volume of poetry made by Barbara Brown, Emily Carty, Professor August "Gus" H. Konkel, The Reverend John F. Lockyer, Neil Paul (Poet Friend), Alison Sauve, Beverly Shepard, Christoph Summer, Niklas Summer, Philipp Summer, and especially, Ed VandenDool for his selection of the graphics that complement the poems.

I wish to thank my family, friends, and teachers (animal, vegetable, and mineral) for the nudges they have given to push me on my way to record my meanderings, meditations, and impressions.

It is my prayer to encourage others to enter into the joy of poetry, "to hold, as 'twere the mirror up to nature."

Sheldon H. Clark, D. Min.
2020

Previous Publications
Poetry and Prayer Sketches, by Sheldon H. Clark, 2013
Voices Extended, by Neil Paul and Sheldon H. Clark, 2016

Still
Voices

Sheldon H. Clark

DEDICATION

To my grandson, Foxlo Clark McPhail,
And, as ever, for Amber and Ryan

In Faith, Hope, and Love

CONTENTS

Endorsements 1
Preface 2
Acknowledgements 3
OPENING PRAYER 7
MUSINGS
    1. Arrived 8
    2. Prison 9
    3. La Morte 10
    4. Unintended Consequences 11
    5. Frontal Headache 12
    6. Sonnet: Go I, debt blind, made poor, but for thy grace 13
NEW TESTAMENT INSPIRATION
    7. The Abbey 14
    8. Patience, *Ye are the light of the world* (Matthew 5:14) 15
    9. Inasmuch (Matthew 25:40) 16
    10. *Old things are passed away* (II Corinthians 5:15) 17
    11. The Gift of God (Ephesians 2:8) 18
    12. He Died Desired to be Forgotten (Matthew 27:33-50; 18-20) 19
    13. The Parable of the Mustard Seed 20
        (Matthew 13:31, 32; Mark 4:31, 32; Luke 13:18,19) ....
    14. Alpha and Omega (Revelation 22:13) 21
OLD TESTAMENT INSPIRATION
    15. Psalm 1 22
    16. Psalm 24 23
    17. Psalm 51 24
    18. Psalm 122 25
CLOSING PRAYERS
    Night Falls on All, by Bayne Cummer 26
    We Thank Thee, by Robert Louis Stevenson 27
APPENDIX
    Psalm 24, *KJV* 28

Let the words of my mouth,
and the meditation of my heart,
be acceptable in thy sight,
O Lord, my strength, and my redeemer.

Psalm 19:14

God of Light and Life,
Thank You for Your guidance
to be accurate,
to be discerning,
to marry our hearts and heads
in writing these poems.

Our desire has been to reflect Your Creation,
and to extend a cordial invitation
to others brave enough
to engage their poetic curiosity
into these meanderings into truth.

Amen

ARRIVED

A waddling gander honked for his mate near the stirred farm pond.
He was concerned; not really anxious.

Another pair just stopped on the lime green weedy approach.
She had flopped down to rest, while he stood sentinel.

The brightening red sky promised sun, darkening clouds forecast rain; cool, then warmth.
Farm work had to be done in, through and around the muck, and above the ankle deep mire.

Almost no time to pause, to take in the overnight-growing grasses, budding trees and bushes,
The disappearing mud puddles, and the cleansing aroma from the gentle breeze.

Animals nickered, mooed, barked, and meowed for their grain, hay, and feed.
A single feral "Tom" insistently baby-cried harbinger of seasonal transition and new life.

Unmistakable were the country signs of the ancient ritual of creation.
God's creatures, earth, waters, crystal clear puffs of cloud moved across sky's dome.

Then, in the faint far-off, human folly spewed testosterone again and again,
As though the good earth could absorb more and more bloody battle scars.

PRISON

This prison is the great globe itself.

It is a prison of seeping noxious gases stampeding mortality.

Simple exposure is death invisible.

Stragglers, followers, leaders alike are transfigured.

The prison is a poisonous contagion isolating and destroying.

Toxic touch, breath, whiffs are the new ecological reality.

This prison is from a cough, a sneeze, or even the proverbial kiss.

Inscape is the source of contagion, not landscape, nor seascape, nor Elysian Fields.

No sight, touch, taste, sound, nor sense can arrest the insatiable relish of death.

This poison prison shrivels God's Images of body, mind, and spirit into mere oblivion.

Where have all the flowers gone?

Where have all the children gone?

"Where be your gibes now? Your gambol? Your songs? Your flashes of merriment?"

Where have all the remnants gone when needed to heal,

to vision immortality, and to make love?

LA MORTE

Human death is usually set in some type of bed.
Irregular breathing
Quiet subdued voices; heart to heart observations, and dimmed light are clichés.
Low blood pressure
The dying approaches detachment each in their way.
Mottling and coldness
Some slip away. Some offer a gesture of protest. All succumb.
Comatose
Mostly, there is no violent struggle.
Agitation

Death is played out in war.
Denial is reality
The young and the brave feel invincible.
Immortal instruments of destiny
Trained to kill is protective like invisible armor.
Hermetically sealed
Accidents happen anywhere anytime unexpectedly.
What?
Adversarial encounters happen in the day and at night.
Human rights and expected civil laws are jettisoned for expediency.

Death that should not be, is not quiet, nor peaceful.
Screams
Hatred, bigotry, racism, prejudice, anger, repugnance, xenophobia describe the case.
Odium
Self-defense and defense of country are radically unalike.
Convulsive
Rules do not apply when determined superior physical force is employed.
Collateral damage
Chaotic ruthless anarchy and peaceful petition are polar opposites.
Listen.
Climate change is coming.

Life matters. Lives matter.
I can't breathe. I can't breathe. I can't breathe.

UNINTENDED CONSEQUENCES

"Shoot a tin can off its perch in the empty car bay."
      No one was around.
"Have some solo fun on this hot August afternoon.
Close the door against danger."
      The first shot ricocheted off the spade bowl,
      broke the ancient garage window,
      poked a hole into the dining room, and spent,
      rested at my brother's feet on the carpet.
          Bang. Crash. Silence.
          Click. Ping. Smash. Scream.
"What have I done?"
      I heard his cry, dropped the gun as though shot.
      I dashed past the bees in the apple tree to the kitchen door.
"What were you thinking?"
"I never dreamed."
      Afterward, we played together in summer shadows near the spring house.
      We had cut out a large Mumbly Peg circle in the sweet dry grass.
      Forgiveness need not be said, mercy was left unspoken.
      Grace embraced us with joy in life and unbroken filial love.

FRONTAL HEADACHE
A Dialogue Between Self and Truth

Self: My head aches below the hair line above the eyes in front of the ears.
Truth: Tension.
Self: I am in a state of emotional, mental, physical, and spiritual disquiet.
Truth: *For in much wisdom is much vexation and those who increase knowledge increase sorrow.*
                                                                                        Ecclesiastes 1:18. NRSV

Self: I am afraid of not being able to do anything.
Truth: *There is no fear in love, but perfect love casts out fear.*   1 John 4:18. NRSV
Self: I am afraid of being dependent, of not accomplishing little tasks, of driving at night, of being revealed as incompetent, uncertain, indecisive, of being utterly and completely impotent.
Truth: *Blessed are the poor in spirit, for theirs is the kingdom of heaven.*   Matthew 5:3. NRSV
Self: I am afraid of running out of money.
Truth: Nearly ½ of the world's population – more than 3 billion people – live on less than $2.50 a day. More than 1.3 billion live in extreme poverty – less than $1.25 a day. 80% of the world population lives on less than $10 a day.*
Self: I am afraid of being abandoned, however unintentionally.
Truth: *In everything do to others as you would have them do to you; for this is the law and the prophets.*   Matthew 7:12. NRSV
Self: I am afraid of future real, or imagined, physical and mental incapacities.
Truth: *So do not worry about tomorrow, for tomorrow will bring worries of its own. Today's trouble is enough for today.*   Matthew 6:34. NRSV
Self: I am afraid of loneliness, of crowds, of my self-inflicted protective masks.
Truth: *Last scene of all, That ends this strange eventful history, is second childishness and mere oblivion, Sans teeth, sans eyes, sans taste, sans everything.*
                                                                  Wm. Shakespeare, As You Like It. Act 2 Sc. 7
Self: Strangely, I am not afraid to die.
Truth: *For I am convinced that neither death, nor life… nor anything else in all creation, will be able to separate us from the love of God in Christ Jesus our Lord.*
                                                                                          Romans 8:38. NRSV

* https://www.dosomething.org/facts/11-facts-about-global-poverty 12/1/2015

SONNET

To be read slowly with a twinkle in one's eye.
Think: Agape, Eros, Philia, Storge, and Caritas.

Go I, debt blind, made poor, but for thy grace.
The rainbow's arch with sun's bright gold enchants
A changing landscape stilled by our love's pace
And scribes the mill, the race, the circumstance.
Horizon is made small by curves well known.
Earth air fire water loose our mortal mission
To move unharnessed toward the growing foam
Off far, then near, then given, then taken passion.

Blue green red lifts our vision earth to heaven
To turn, to be upon 'the ancient journey.'
Earth bound, the root, the source of Cupid's leaven,
Enshrines in us this time, this shape, our story.

Look, see, encircled arms embrace true hearts -
The beat, the rhythm, the passion, *a la carte*.

THE ABBEY

Monk ghost shadows flirt with rain shine.
Cold shivers escape as dawn's break harkens
To an affectionate, inviting aura.
Silence dons masonry with fecund aromas
Casually drifting, lifting with the gentle breeze
Skeletal tree tops to the blue-grey above.

A remembered choir chants the processional litany
Of an echo down the age worn aisle stones.
They sway to separate at the chancel crossing to
Epistle side and Gospel side and disappear.

Purity, Summary of the Law, Readings,
Offertory, Intercessions, Spiritual Openings,
Absolution, Thanksgiving, Christ's Memorial,
Request for God's Mercy, Communion, *Pater Noster*,
Adoration, Blessing, and the Invitation to Service
Fill the open wondering eyes, ears, nostrils, tongues, hands and hearts.

What vision just disappeared into the mists?
Recall the Recessional. Stay the moment Divine. Beckon us over the chasm.
Let us escape the temporal and become at one with the Immortal
Free from the primal forces of self-preservation and tribal affiliation.

For just a moment Temporality lifts and transports
Us, suspended in time and space,
Elevated to another dimension
Beyond earthly knowledge or apprehension
Beyond cause and effect
Assumed in an atmosphere we are blessed to breathe.

Monk ghost shadows flirt with rain shine.
Cold shivers escape as dawn's break harkens
To an affectionate, inviting aura
Silence dons masonry with fecund aromas
Casually drifting, lifting with the gentle breeze
Skeletal tree tops to the blue-grey above.

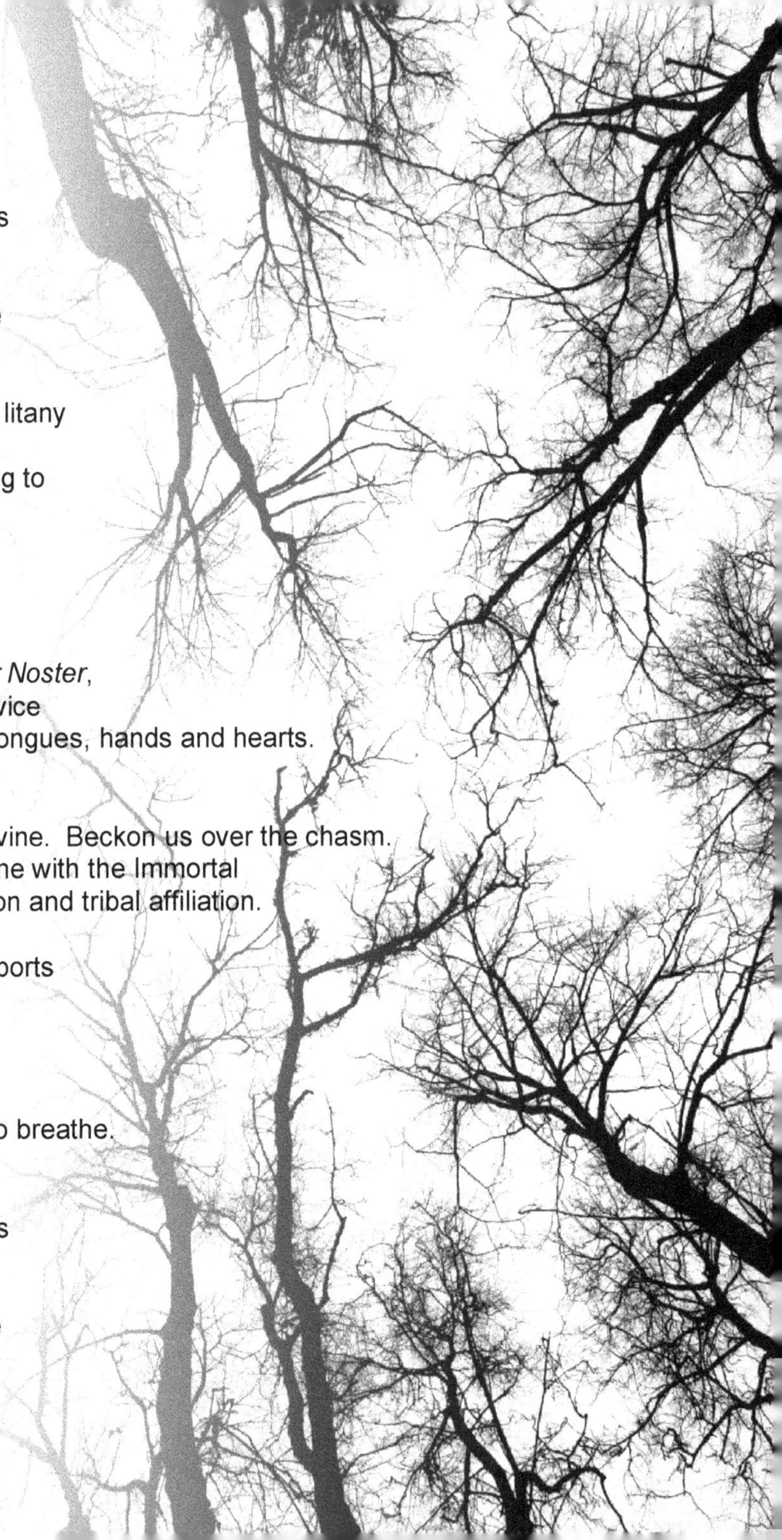

PATIENCE
Ye are the light of the world.

Matthew 5:14.

Pichanur Village, Coimbatore District, South India

Patience is not just a personal quality of reserve, or a card game to be played alone.
It is the virtue to take time each day to set aside the day's worried cares.
It is the discipline to take the time to be present in the Eternal Now with loved ones.

Mr. Krishnaswami sat on his open freshly dried dung scrubbed porch stoop.
His required teacher's tie was purposely relegated to the porch bench.
His white uniform pants had been changed to a simple dhoti.
His after work call to patience was directed to the gentle bouncing of the baby on his knee.

Patiently, the father lifted the babe up and down, and then
He shifted the dynamic balance to left and right and up and down.
Smiling laughter welled up from the father and son conspirators in the cool shaded warmth.

Patiently, the mother joined in their smiles as she made tea and stirred rice and vegetable curry.
She loved this time of motherhood relief, of aromatic meal preparation, of hearth and home.
She relaxed and enjoyed the scene between their game play and her cooking fire.

Patiently, this holy family acted out its familial love scene.
They were unaware of the single shepherd bystander who spontaneously smiles with them.
They were absorbed in this moment of peace, of hope for the future, of future possibilities.

No, Patience is not just a personal quality of reserve, or a card game to be played alone.
Patience describes every family in our global village striving to grow old together in the hope
That Tagore's dream of freedom without fear, good health, enough to eat, education, and purpose
would be universally attained.

Where the mind is without fear and the head is held high;
Where knowledge is free;
Where the world has not been broken up into fragments by domestic walls;
Where words come out from the depth of truth;
Into that heaven of freedom, my Father, let my country awake.

Rabindranath Tagore
1861-1941

INASMUCH
Matthew 25:40

Inasmuch is a cutting word.

    The buck saw worked through the seasoned wood, the Word that was to fire.

Inasmuch is a calling to serve.

    The cut wood heated the bustle and the wassail of communion, the rising bread.

Inasmuch is a yearning to be gifted outright.

    The smell, the taste of apple, cinnamon, cloves, and honey distilled patient spirits.

Inasmuch brought God's peace.

    The embers were left smoldering.

Inasmuch answered heart whispers in the melded malt and in the baking bread.

    They laughed and then fell silent in the gathering Light to the crackling warmth within.

**OLD THINGS ARE PASSED AWAY;
BEHOLD, ALL THINGS ARE BECOME NEW.**

II Corinthians 5:17

First Day is every day. It is the Lord's Day.   It is our day.
Penitents kneel in the presence of the mystery of God's Truth.
"Old things are passed away; behold, all things are become new."

Open heart surgery is a matter of choice. Death is a real possibility.
One's earthly will for God's sake is preparation for right ordering.
Material matters are immaterial to life restoration itself.

Surgical skill, measures, deftness, freezes timeless in the intensity of the moment.
A life is at stake. Concentration accelerating efficiency is paramount.
Attention, eyes, ears, hands, bodies, and hearts focus.
Incision is precise, swift, and sufficient.
Light and apparatus are needed and activated.
Surgery unfolds the drama this time as though for the first time.
Step by step, moment by moment happens in precise lock step wonder.
Precision anchored by care preserves still another life.
The breath of life restores a living soul.

Wonder, faith, hope, and love
Transform prayers into stirrings.
Anesthetic numbness gives way to memory, acknowledgement and gratitude.

The Light of the Spirit burns ever brighter.
The Light of the Spirit brings a time of thanksgiving.
The Light of the Spirit speaks to headwaters, waterfalls, and living streams.

I am who I am.
Renewed life is conscious of God's gift of being, gazing into Eternity.
"Old things are passed away; behold, all things are become new."

THE GIFT OF GOD

*For by grace you have been saved through faith,
and this is not your own doing; it is the gift of God.*
Ephesians 2:8 (NRSV)

Good versus Evil is The Garden distinction.
Contrasting values are forged by word and action,
Music and theatre, dance and art, work and sacramental ritual.

Light versus Dark is a competitive illusion
Juxtaposed is the Spirit of Truth against the limitation of Materiality
Not able to be reconciled by earthly endeavors.

Enter God's Grace and Love,
Not two, but One Spirit
Miraculously unifying that which seems irreconcilable.

Spirit answers Spirit
In an eternal circle of generosity and astonishment.
It is humanly incomprehensible, but spiritually perpetually believable.

Spirit accomplishes the unimaginable.
Spirit releases from within the human soul
Willing choices to be just, merciful, and humble.

The gift of God is Grace.
Grace, unmerited forgiveness, transcends.
Grace opens the human spirit blessed by the Divine Spirit.

Amen.

HE DIED DESIRED TO BE FORGOTTEN

He died desired to be forgotten.
Stripped of His life
He wandered in future tombs of
Millenniums of memories.

Idol sculptors enshrined
His image in adorned wood, stone and with
Gems set in silver and gold:
Commercial presentations
Rendering His Catharsis.

The two hung there:
One left, one right
The quick and the dead.
Future.
Forgotten.
Present.

That Noon time of night He moved.
Moonlit shadow shades
Not quite under
The vault's overhang,
He lay wrapped naked,
A grotesque solitude of Body,
Not of Spirit,
Uniquely qualified.
"He is risen."

Outcasts meet
In and through Him,
Perpetually.

In Love, He called from the Cosmos,
Get up, my children
Become with me.
Resurrected,
He lives.

Amen.

THE PARABLE OF THE MUSTARD SEED

Matthew 13:31, 32   Mark 4:31, 32   Luke 13:18, 19

The Second Adam sowed mustard seed in a field.

The seeds' husks held the power of potential extravagance.

Potent grains to dispel death, decay, darkness, enmity, evil, fear, limitation.

Potent grains to dispense love, joy, peace, goodness, faith, meekness, temperance.

The mustard tree emerged from darkness to Light.

Rooted firmly, it sprouted to magnificent stature.

The seeds endings marked the openings for abundance.

Joyful songsters miraculously alighted, rested, built, and raised their young.

Then, they flitted away, and away, and ever back again.

They announced the Good News: God is good.

Amen.

ALPHA AND OMEGA

Adam and Eve loved God's Garden.
God's wisdom anchored goodness in love.

The two loved paradise.
Exploration revealed infinite probabilities of engagement.

God left them alone, unwinking.
The seed to astonish had been sown.

Goodness, truth, beauty over-arched God's creation.
Adam and Eve basked in the primeval surround.

Freely, together and apart, they meandered.
Sniffing, savoring, seeing, stirring, heeding, they knew bliss.

God's creation provoked tears of laughter and joy.
Natural curiosity gave birth to the seductive fruit of victory.

"We are truly with God."
God's approval for newfound comprehension was not meant to be.

Original knowledge foreshadowed fatal disobedience.
Adam's and Eve's exit from divine space annealed God's love.

The Garden of God's love closed.
Curiosity brought finality.

The second Adam restored God's love.
Blessed are the pure in heart: for they shall see God.

PSALM 1

God's peace is known not by humans
   Who trudge in deserts of covetous deceit, and
   Who are trapped by subversive choices.

Divine Presence is found when the Beloved
   Listens to God's soul-reviving beckoning.

God's love is as powerful as an artesian well spring,
   And as restorative as spiritual cure.
   Harvesters of nourishing ingathering obey
   the Spirit, and flourish in transcendent abundance.

Humans, trapped in selfishness are like scythed
   wheat strewn by merciless winds.

God knows that the way of unrighteousness leads to
   alienation.

God knows and accepts the Beloved intimately, but
   forsakes those who choose to disobey God's
   Holy Ordinances.

PSALM 24 *

This is God's creation and everything that inhabits it.

This is God's world, created from a sea of mystery, and celebrated for its munificence.

What human beings ever dare approach God, or even have the timidity to be in God's Holy presence?

Only those rare persons who have emptied themselves of deceit and pride

Shall they be blessed and find salvation.

Only those who seek God's will, and obey it as if it was their own, shall be blessed.

God shall enter into his people, his living temples, and be glorified.

Who is this God of Creation? God is the ultimate source of Love and Compassion.

God shall enter into his people, his living temples, and be glorified.

Who is this God of Creation? God is the ultimate source of Love and Compassion.

* see appendix

Psalm 51
A Psalm of David

Out of your merciful compassion and out of your tender mercies,
O God, baptize me afresh in conscience and in spirit from the sins of lust and covetous.
Wash me, scrub me, and bleach out my heinousness crimes, my wickedness.

I know I have succumbed to the passions of desire and have committed premeditated murder.
My spirit is imprisoned by prevalent guiltiness.
I have sinned against God, against God's Holy ordinances.
Sinfulness is my inheritance. I am ashamed.
God, you have every reason to judge and condemn me.

Even my birth was preceded by predominant sinfulness.
God, you desire to infuse my being, my very soul with wisdom.

Cleanse me. Purify me whiter than new fallen snow.
I plead with you, O God, to know your ecstasy. Heal my broken bones.

Do not identify my most grievous sins as heralds of eternal damnation.
Cleanse me from all evil. Create in me a clean heart. Renew my soul.

Do not deny me your presence. Imbue me with your Holy Spirit.
Grant me new life. I shall become an example of God's grace-filled spirit.

I shall be your messenger to instruct others to obey your commandments.
They, too, will become your disciples.
Remove from my inmost being my guiltiness, and I shall be an instrument of your peace.

Help me speak your truths and proclaim the glories of your creation.
You spurn sacrifices and burnt offerings.

My sacrifices to you are a subdued spirit; an obedient and contrite heart for your acceptance.
O God, I plead with you to be compassionate toward Israel, and help her build your New Jerusalem.

It is then, O God that you will be pleased with our symbolic offerings, sacrifices and oblations
as we tender them to your glory.

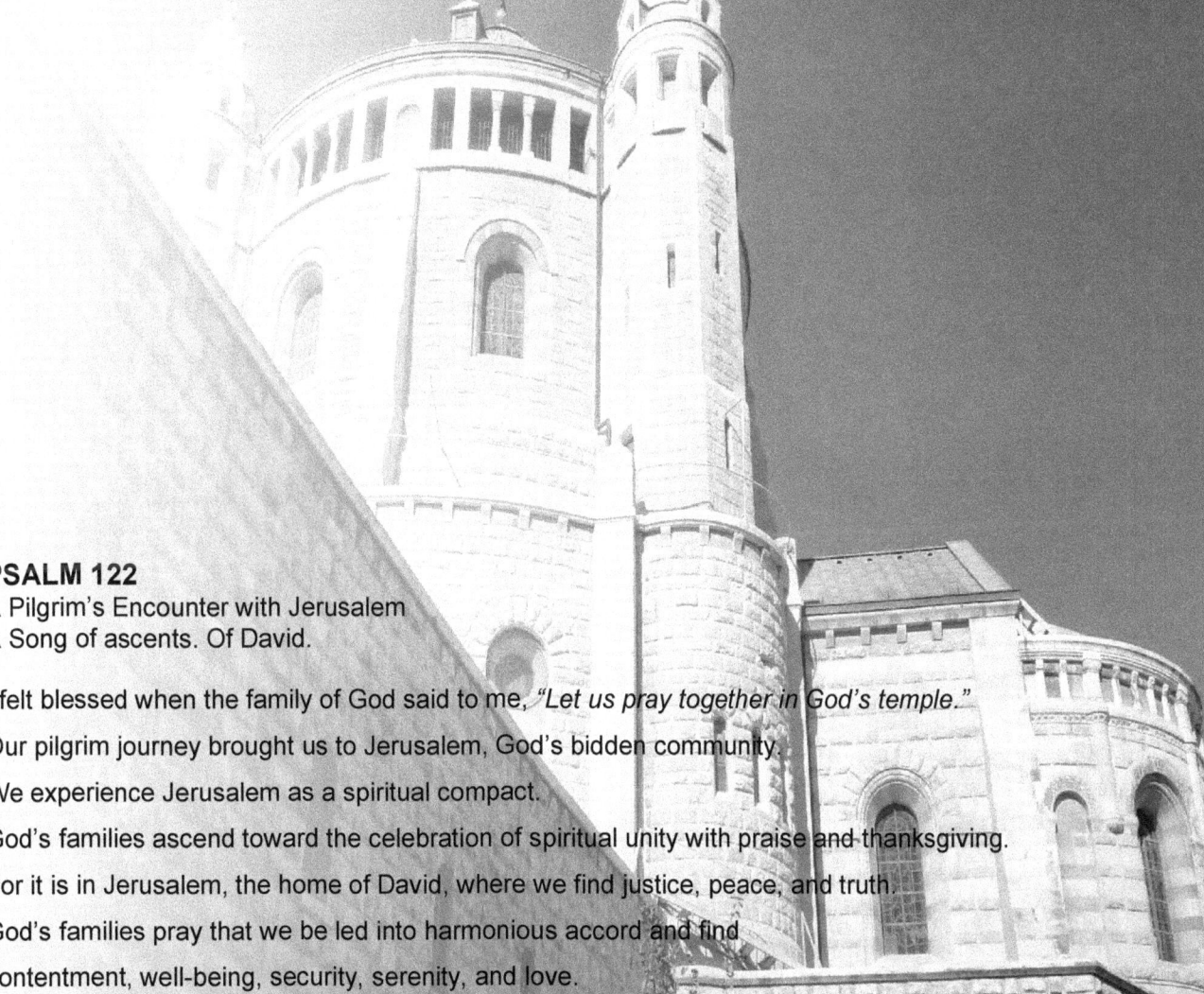

PSALM 122
A Pilgrim's Encounter with Jerusalem
A Song of ascents. Of David.

I felt blessed when the family of God said to me, *"Let us pray together in God's temple."*

Our pilgrim journey brought us to Jerusalem, God's bidden community.

We experience Jerusalem as a spiritual compact.

God's families ascend toward the celebration of spiritual unity with praise and thanksgiving.

For it is in Jerusalem, the home of David, where we find justice, peace, and truth.

God's families pray that we be led into harmonious accord and find contentment, well-being, security, serenity, and love.

We pray as one for God's loving-kindness to saturate everyone, everywhere, and in everything.

We pray to God for God's love to transform us, so that we may truly say, *"Peace be within you."*

God's families pray to God for its communal welfare and for God's mercy, love, truth, and peace.

NIGHT FALLS ON ALL

Night falls on all, yet our high thoughts,
our holy devotions and our steadfast loves
shall live from age to age, from eternity to eternity.
They shall not die, though all else sink into decay and oblivion,
for they are woven of an immortal texture
that the breath of forgetfulness may never mar.

Bayne Cummer
Pickering College Student, 1927-1929

Nota Bene:
Pickering College Headmaster Joe McCulley (1927-1948) was sent **Night Falls on All**, by Bayne Cummer's parents after his untimely death in the summer of 1929. **Night Falls on All** has been a part of Pickering College lore ever since.

WE THANK THEE

Lord, behold our family here assembled.
We thank Thee for this place in which we dwell;
for the love that unites us;
for the peace accorded us this day;
for the hope with which we expect the morrow;
for the health, the work, the food, and the bright skies,
that make our lives delightful;

and for our friends in all parts of the earth.
Let peace abound in our small company.
Purge out of every heart the lurking grudge.
Give us grace and strength to forbear and to persevere.
Give us the grace to accept and to forgive offenders.
Forgetful ourselves, help us to bear cheerfully
    the forgetfulness of others.
Give us courage and gaiety and the quiet mind.
Spare to us our friends, soften to us our enemies.
Bless us, if it may be, in all our innocent endeavors.
If it may not, give us the strength to encounter
    that which is to come,
that we be brave in peril, constant in tribulation,
    temperate in wrath,
and in all changes of fortune, and, down to the gates of death,
    loyal and loving one to another.

                                    Robert Louis Stevenson
                                          1850-1894

APPENDIX

Psalm 24 KJV

The earth is the LORD's, and the fullness thereof; the world, and they that dwell therein.

For he hath founded it upon the seas, and established it upon the floods.

Who shall ascend into the hill of the LORD? or who shall stand in his holy place?

He that hath clean hands, and a pure heart;

Who hath not lifted up his soul unto vanity, nor sworn deceitfully.

He shall receive the blessing from the LORD, and righteousness from the God of his salvation.

This is the generation of them that seek him, that seek thy face, O Jacob.

Selah.

Lift up your heads, O ye gates; and be ye lift up, ye everlasting doors;

And the King of glory shall come in.

Who is this King of glory?

The LORD strong and mighty, the LORD mighty in battle.

Lift up your heads, O ye gates; even lift them up, ye everlasting doors;

And the King of glory shall come in.

Who is this King of glory?

The LORD of hosts, he is the King of glory.

Selah.

www.ingramcontent.com/pod-product-compliance
Lightning Source LLC
Chambersburg PA
CBHW051121110526
44589CB00026B/2996